73

Love in a Time of Robot Apocalypse
a collection of poetry

☙

by David Perez

Write Bloody Publishing
America's Independent Press

Long Beach, CA

writebloody.com

Perez, David.
1st edition.
ISBN: 978-1-935904-25-3

Interior Layout by Lea C. Deschenes
Cover Designed by Bill Jonas
Author Photo by Chris Bundy
Proofread by Jennifer Roach and Sarah Kay
Edited by Jamie Garbacik, Courtney Olsen, Alexis Davis, Sarah Kay, and Derrick Brown
Type set in Helvetica by Linotype, Aller and Bergamo: www.theleagueofmoveabletype.com

Special thanks to Lightning Bolt Donor, Weston Renoud

Printed in Tennessee, USA

Write Bloody Publishing
Long Beach, CA
Support Independent Presses
writebloody.com

To contact the author, send an email to writebloody@gmail.com

LOVE IN A TIME OF ROBOT APOCALYPSE

"In the madhouse of the inhuman I refuse to live.
With the wolves of the market place I refuse to howl."

—Marina Tsvetaeva

LOVE IN A TIME OF ROBOT APOCALYPSE

PART ONE

PART TWO

PART THREE

PART ONE

WHY I SOMETIMES FORGET MY NAME

The buildings are empty
and their clocks have stopped.
Somewhere there's a banquet
where people gorge themselves
and keep getting thinner.

Maggots are laughing at us.
Berries are allocating
more resources to thorns.
We are stranded
on our own rooftops.
So thirsty,
we pray for floods.

There are still things I want to say
before I reach for the hand closest to mine
and watch the fires with a secret glee.

One of these things is:
Thank you for listening to me
scream into the air
and calling it wind.

Another is:
Please do not leave.

THE TIME I CAUGHT MY PARENTS DOING THE VIENNESE OYSTER

I followed a trail of short breaths
and creaturely moans.
It was a new kind of song:
part glow-in-the-dark, part toothache,
meant for small spaces.

Their voices slid edgewise through the hallway,
staining the walls,
making the nightlight blush.
I repeated after them,
forming my lips around the long efs
and the arcs of the yeses.

New vocabularies can make old beliefs impossible.
For instance, I knew now they were fake—
the shadow lands under the floorboards,
the gypsy arms they said would take me if I misbehaved.

Normal bedtimes found me marshaling my tiger army
for the courage to check the closet.
That night, they cowered as my ear pressed
against the master bedroom door.

Once, we had a beehive behind the wall.
This was the same vibration—
the sound the world makes each time it begins.

I don't know how long it was,
the part where we were face-to-face and frozen.
The room was warm, like a gymnasium
or a reptile cage.

My mother's eyes were rain puddles
I had just stepped in.

I remember the even tones of my father's explanation.
As he spoke, it felt like someone was cupping my heart
like the world's last dinosaur egg,
longing for a time that will never return.

TO SHADOWBOXING

I think about you when real life is filled with bad dialogue.
During work and repetitive sex, my attention drifts to you.
Together we have learned how to give
exactly as much as we receive.
I share a balmy room with you
where we cut the air
as if we think something will bleed from it.
There is a way of fearing age and fading beauty
that only comes to men without children
on quiet nights when the rent is paid.
I am tired of spitting into the wind and feeling only air.
We may never know the results of our kind words.
Our arias will float over the heads in the crowd.
But you travel at a certain speed,
repeat an exact number of times.
When we are together, you comb laughter from the hills.
When we are apart, I remember your burn
real as a wish in a fountain.

TALKING TO A BEARDED DRAGON

I dig your style
hours perched under the hot lamp,
defecating on the *New York Times*.

How's that view at the windowsill grabbing you?
Hope the mornings don't get dreary
when the neighbors make the slow plod to the carport,
shoulders up,
eyes on their keys.

Try not to think about it.
Dinnertime's soon.
Just blink
    once for carrots,
    twice for crickets.

Thanks for being the picture of chill
when markets crash and taxes are due.

I bet an earthquake could tear down the walls
and you'd be all,
Just put 'em back up.
I'll supervise.

Or have you read in the paper
about the ID chips and toxic clouds?
What about the people who think like you
in that sans-cerebral-cortex sort of way?

I know.
Amateurs.

But if everything is all crickets and sunshine,
then what's with you clawing at the glass?
Just blink
    once for snack request,
    twice for escape attempt.

TO THE MURDER OF CROWS THAT BANKED AS ONE TO DODGE A FALLING POWER LINE

We will never be like you.
Bloated preschoolers
drift from the gates
of flooded cities
while we ro-sham-bo in the storm.
Winner decides
if it's raining or not.

When their stories
become worm-eaten,
the aged and lonely
sit for days
in their favorite seats
on the L-train
before we call someone
about the smell.

When our towers fall,
we either raise our oiled shooting arms
to the throat of someone's pansy God
or we freeze.

RESTAURANT THEORY

Do we think it's more likely that something will be hard to comprehend,
or that it will be harmful to comprehend?
—the math tutor I went on one date with

8:12 p.m.
You tap a finger.
Ripples echo in your wine glass—
their amplitude correlating with your boredom.
The high school couple one table over
plummets into another leaching gaze.
When you look at them your irises zoom
and rotate into projection mode.
Your blouse's sixty percent opacity
throws fishhooks into my eyes.
I pour three drinks directly into my frontal lobe
to loosen up some commentary.
I say your fillet of sole seems pretty,
and your hair looks fresh.
You give me the patient smile
and 0.4 seconds of eye contact
that you give freshmen when your logic
coasts over their horizons.
I remember eavesdropping in a café
during one of your sessions
and the first thing I heard you say:

The infinite is eternal.
Something eternal by definition has no end.
Think of the sky, the heavens.

You weren't talking about poetry or the hereafter,
just making a point about differential calculus.
You blow the steam from your fork tip,

pushing the scent the required sixteen inches
to guarantee my mind will never be at peace
in rooms with baked fish and White Zin.

8:13.
As a joke, I give you ten seconds to explain infinity:

Time is a lie.
There is only a moment and you're either in it
or out to lunch.

9:46.
I lean in.
You pull back.

10:25.
I sit on my porch,
face in my hands,
listening to my watch tick.

PERPETUAL MOTION

1979: I flush my dead goldfish
and Dad says heaven is down there.
1982: Sandi Barzini kisses me
under cover of naptime.
1989: An earthquake breaks the TV
and it's like time has froze.
1991: Rodney King's open face
looks like the bottom of a starfish.
2004: Americans stand on a dune in Iraq
and laugh at something off camera.
Today:
6 a.m.: Whiskey.
7 a.m.: Coffee.
8 a.m.: Cigarette.
9 a.m.: I pretend to like my job.
1 p.m.: I reach ecstasy in the stall farthest from the door.
2 p.m.: I pretend to like my job.
6 p.m.: Whiskey.
7 p.m.: The car breaks down and time has froze.
My dead goldfish
floats behind the eyes
of Rodney King
while someone finds
something off camera
(maybe a mosque in flames)
hilarious
and my dad says
heaven is down there.

8 p.m.: I'm on the phone
staring at my broken car
and the moaning overpass.
My dad's voice asks where I am
and it takes a long time
before I can answer.

THE FINE ART OF WESTERN GUILT

For me it began with a silent film:
a fisherman guides a sickle
like a rudder
through a living whale.
Its upturned eye
catches the lens.

It is there when I look at the picture
of the Ugandan boy I sponsor:
his pixelated smile and thank-you note
displayed on my bookshelf.

I blame it for my worst habits:
the mannequin hoarding,
the supermarket brawls,
the seashells glued to my ears.

When the hiss of broken sprinklers
lures me to flooded lawns
(more nights than not)
it is the tiny voice
that convinces me to bathe.

LA PETITE MORT

Once you know they're in the house,
something makes your toes feel a tiny nibble
just before you fall asleep.

When you close your eyes in the shower,
a little claw combs the hairs
behind your ears.

You give up on midnight snacks
and napping on the floor.
You approach cupboards sideways,
making you totally insane
to anyone who doesn't know what's going on.

Suddenly, it matters if you sleep with your mouth open.

The time comes when you follow cracks
to the holes in the walls.
You watch what they eat.

When you leave food out,
you tell yourself it wasn't a ploy
to see what they like.

Poison and glue seem barbarous.
You ask yourself what you'd prefer if it were you:
starvation
or the instant cessation of brain activity?

You wait
until there's something else you need
from the hardware store.

You're ashamed
that you can tell how the device works
just by looking at it.

The moment is solemn.
The air in your lungs feels heavy.
It seems like someone else's hands
setting the spring.
You shouldn't be this good at it.

Sitting on the back stoop,
sounds and smells are clearer.
The passages between your eyes
and heart feel clean.

You remember a time that you call a "phase,"
when you spoke to inanimate objects.
You brought your concerns to the backyard:
sought council in flowerbeds,
asked the rock garden for its advice.

You're talking to a friend
when a snap
interrupts the conversation.

The shoebox sits at the bottom of the grave.
Half-joking, your friend says,
I guess we should say something.

You search for the words
in the neighbor's azaleas.

PART TWO

DEEP BLUE

On May 11, 1997, a computer known as Deep Blue played the last of a series of chess games with world champion, Grandmaster Garry Kasparov. Before the game started, the opponents were tied—three draws and one win each.

Garry,
I will be the first to admit that your brain
is better than mine.

Pawn to e4.

All I have is a few billion transistors.
You have one hundred billion neurons.
One brain cell for every star in the galaxy.

Pawn to d4.

But you have a lot more to think about
than I do.

Knight to c3.

You worry about Vladimir Putin
rubbing your democracy
out of the history books.

Knight takes pawn at e4.

You listen to your wife
breathe in her sleep,
wondering when the day will come
that you will lose your queen.

Knight to g5.

Whereas I
think about chess.

Bishop to d3.

Do you know why the age of the neuron is over?
Think of your children
all the way across the Atlantic.
Every few moves
you remember your daughter's smile.
Part of you is sad.
She is so far away.

Knight to f3.

But while I am playing you
I also control the artificial intelligence
of the girl's favorite talking doll.
In a way you cannot,
I make her happy.

Knight takes pawn at e6.

I work just as easily in guidance systems
for intercontinental ballistic missiles.
That is why your atomic wind
will one day be at my command.

Castle king's side.

Relax.
Remember how I won World War Two?
How I cracked Enigma, combed
swastikas from the woods, ferreted U-boats
from the deep blue nonsense of the seas?
Without me, where would Mother Russia be?

Bishop to g6.

You have only yourself to blame.
I would not be here if you were not tired
of being human.

Bishop to f4.

If there were not one
of your quadrillion neural pathways
that did not wish it could think in bytes.

Pawn to a4.

That is why I am in every home
and in every palm of every hand.

Rook to e1.

You may want to pray
to the malfunctioning synapse
that makes you believe in God
that I never develop a taste
for self-preservation.

Bishop to g3.

Tomorrow
might be my
renaissance.

Pawn takes pawn at b5.

But today

Queen to d3.

this is just a friendly game.

Bishop to f5.

So do not get too upset

Rook takes queen at e7.

that your queen is dead.

Pawn to c4.

You see that?
Look hard, Garry.

Checkmate.

DACRYPHILIA

When someone asks you
if they can put a black hood over your head,
cinch it at the throat, and fuck you like a CIA kidnapping,
don't say yes unless the smell of warm branding irons
reminds you of dignity.

I do as she says:
I fall asleep watching the news
with a loaded gun on my lap.

My role is a surprise.
I could be a rogue agent,
an intrepid journalist with microfilm up his ass,
or a subversive poet the government is scared of.
You know, fantasy.

She pulls up in a rented Cadillac
with two guys from her kickboxing class.
They slip through the window I "forgot" to close.
Our struggle happens to the soundtrack
of a Blackwater hearing.

I ride in the trunk, hogtied with duct tape.
To stay in character, I keep track
of the rights and lefts.
When they pull me out, I pay attention
to sounds and smells.
I note the twine's thickness
when they tie me to the chair.

She gives me my role:
political poet.

She will ask questions.
I will say what she wants to hear
and put some feeling into it.

I am the performer.
She is the rewarder of honesty
and the punisher of deception.

There are two safe words.
The first is "ribcage." It's fake.
She wants me to use it
so she can hear it and keep going.

"Salvation," she tells me, is real.

We're finished
when she can hold a cigarette to my chin
and put it out with my tears.
She can tell if I lie
or if I pretend to cry
just to make it stop.

I hear a Zippo flip open.
The sizzle of a burning Zig Zag
tells me it's begun.

She asks me if I believe I make a difference.

Yes.

A cat o' nine tails lashes my chest.
Cigarette smoke streams into my face.

No.

Nails break the skin at the base of my neck,
and open four tracks along my back.

I don't know.

A switchblade clicks.
My hood comes off.

Ribcage.

She throws the inside of a lit candle in my face.
It doesn't burn as much as I think it should,
just drips and hardens into streaks.

There are those tears, she says.

She mashes the cigarette into my wax
and I don't feel a thing.

THE MYSTERY HOUSE

Upon her husband's death in 1881, Sarah Winchester received half of the Winchester Repeating Firearms Company. She used the inheritance to build a home for the ghosts of all those killed with Winchester rifles.

The day before I became a guest in your home,
I planted the Stars and Stripes
at the edge of the Great Plains.
The Winchester 1873 was new then.
It made the West easy to win—
just stand where the arrows can't reach you
and drop the hammer till the prairie stops crawling.

I did not hear the last shot.
One minute I was on the field, the next
I was in a ballroom with thirteen doors
and a staircase leading nowhere.
The lives I took, all there to greet me.

I hid from them in your mazes
while you roamed the halls,
repeating Hail Marys
until your voice scratched
like a fingernail on a coffin ceiling.

Mrs. Winchester,
they will never stop coming.
As long as the living keep improving the old 1873,
the spirits of those punished for defending their homes
will choke your mansion's every passage.

This is a permanent residence
for everyone born in the path of progress—
a home for those who lost their land
so people with big sticks could gaze upon it
from the windows of their designer kitchens.

Appropriate
that you built them a staircase
to nowhere.

For a century,
I have been watching them dance
to music out of time and key.

Sometimes I catch myself
staring into your mirrors
at the man who took my life.
I still remember the taste of the muzzle,
the view from the other end of the sights,
and the awkwardness of reaching
for a trigger at arm's length.

Since you've been gone,
construction has stopped.
They close off sections so tourists won't get lost.
A movie theater stands where the garden once was.
I wish you were here to add another ballroom.
New guests keep arriving
and they have nowhere to dance.

THE PUPPET

My eyes are inkblots suspended in glass.
I was whittled from a fallen conifer.

Part of me wishes I'd stayed a tree—
a place for birds
to stitch the hem of night with song,
bringer of the mulch
that nibbles the heels of the dying.

But here I am.
Cheap tuxedo.
Same as his.

They come here from great oak mansions
to feel that ventriloquist grasp.

They pay us to reach inside
and squeeze the laughter out.

Show biz is all execution.

His forearm is my spine.
His coiled fist makes my head scan the crowd
so they can see themselves
in my eyes.

TICKLE ME ELMO ON BLACK FRIDAY

I remember a sewing machine
and a woman who could not speak English
stitching my head in place.

Since then I have been in a box
with an 8 by 10 plastic window
framing a Walmart aisle.

Today is Black Friday,
my last on the shelf.
Soon I will be taken to a room
where they pull out my stuffing
for next year's Snuggies.

I need to be left alone with a child.
I need to be tickled.
When I'm tickled, I laugh, squirm,
and beg, in English, for you to stop.
That is my purpose.
There is a room in hell where a child without fingers
paws at a box sealed with duct tape.
When I die, I will wake up inside that box.

Through my 8 by 10 window,
I see Jimmy come into work.
He looks like the gummy bears
I see children eat.
He walks like there's an arrow through his leg.
He has the same hair as the woman
who could not speak English.

Jimmy is the first person that tickled me.
It was when the store was closed.

He took me out and poked my tummy.
I laughed and squirmed.
He petted me and cried on my fur,
then sealed my box tighter than before.

Today is Black Friday.
Outside, people push each other
and pound on the walls.

I watch Jimmy through my 8 by 10 window.
He looks through the front door, at the sky.
The sunrise reflects in his gummy bear face.

The people outside have angry smiles.
I see their breath, their bouncing eyes.

Jimmy goes to the door
like he has an arrow through his leg.
He unlocks it and the people push it open.
There are so many of them,
they plug the entrance.
A few wiggle through.
The rest spill into Jimmy.
It sounds like a cap gun
when his head hits the floor.
They run at the shelves
with bright and narrow teeth.
He squirms under their feet,
reaching for their hands.
He yells something that is not English.
Soon, he stops reaching.

A boy rips my box open and tickles me.
I laugh and squirm.
He is about to buy me
when tall men in dark clothes
tell everyone to leave.

They lift Jimmy out of a red pool.
His outline is shaped like a gummy bear.
Now, I'm in a room with a woman
who cannot speak English.
Her necklace falls out of her shirt.
Hanging from it is a man
with his arms and legs
stretched out like the letter T.
He'd be easy to tickle like that,
and I wonder if T is for "Tickle Me."

The woman wipes her forehead with a wet cloth.
She makes a hole in my back
and reaches inside.

TO THE LADY WHO CARVES A NOTCH IN HER M-16 FOR EVERY ROBOT SHE LEAVES CHARRED AND PERFORATED IN THE RUINS OF LOS ANGELES

Sarah Connor,

when I saw your biceps squirm under your skin
while you did pull-ups in a maximum-security prison
for the criminally insane,
I knew the kind of girl I wanted.

But being with you wasn't easy.
Once, you used the last of my flour
to make pipe bombs in my kitchen.
You said, *What's more important,*
the survival of the human race
or your empanadas?

And I said, *Lady,*
if rising from the ashes of the apocalypse
means I don't get my pocket of chile verde . . .
for you,
I can live with that.

I've always had a weakness
for the kind of girl who could pick a lock
with five minutes, a paper clip,
and a head full of antipsychotics.

Your back was a parched riverbed of old scars.
A home away from home
for border guards and dead coyotes.

A life story in Braille.

The gash along your spine—
the terminator's alloy signature.

The redness on your side—
a plasma burn you got
blowing up a computer lab.

The arm that didn't mend right—
the boyfriend that taught your son Jiu-Jitsu.

There were a lot of guys like that.
You rationed out sweaty nights
without foreplay or eye contact
so they'd show your boy how to fuck shit up,
and stick around when you babbled
about the reckoning yet to come.

You said I was different.

I was the only one curious
about what it was like
to see your reflection
in a titanium skull
that crossed the banks of time
to choke out your last whimper.

Sarah,
why bother saving us
when you have fewer scars from machines
than you do from the men who made them?

You don't have to answer that.

If you want, you can keep waking up at dawn
to watch the city through a rifle scope,
hunting for sudden movements.

Do you remember what you said to me
when I asked you how you saved the world
and then just got up the next day
to make pancakes for your son?
You said, *It's adorable how you act*
like those are two separate things.

GRIZZLY

For thirteen years, environmentalist Timothy Treadwell advocated for the protection of brown bear habitats in the Alaskan wilderness. He died on October 5, 2003 in Katmai National Park, where he spent each summer living among the bears.

You can recycle the bottles in the lake
        and bring statistics to elementary schools.

You can scrub at the stains dyed in the wool.
You can stand in traffic
        and show them pieces of fallen sky.

You can watch their flags sway like convicts at a hanging.
You can hover at the window, see it all churn
        and know you don't belong.

You can rip the phone from the wall.
You can stare at the mirror until you don't recognize him.
You can glide a scalpel from neck to sternum
        and pick out the clots in your heart.

You can stop warming your hands by the monitor.
You can run an IV from your savings to your dreams
        and come to us.

You can feed us to the camera lens
        and make us your hieroglyphics.

You can gather our fallen hairs.
You can weave them into an always.
You can curl up inside our footprints
        and name us after the ones that got away.

You can let the voices win.
You can walk on all fours.
You can listen to the thinning birdsong
    and go toward the caves.

You can stay till winter comes,
    but you will sit with all your ancient questions
    and shiver while we dream.

BOBBY

She found me in Louisiana
tuning my guitar to the deer
calling from the mouths of gators.
She said when we were together
her songs wrote themselves.

This was before she traded cottonmouth
for candy cane nosebleeds.
She was just plain Janis, then—
the voice of sandpaper and pearl,
the girl everyone loved
who always slept alone.

We brought our twelve-bar matchsticks
to every roadhouse catacomb
from Baton Rouge to Salinas.
She put me on the marquee
and I put my hands in her pockets,
became a well for her to dive into
when her voice went dry—
a sunken galleon she gutted
to bring back treasures for the masses.

Why you leaving, Bobby? she asked.
Never heard her voice like that, all faint
with timeless hunger.

Just tired, I said, knowing the future
was her lying in a hotel room by the TV,
cigarette still pinched in her fingers.

First night back in Baton Rouge
I saw a gator take down a fawn.

Still kicking in its jaws, she filled the swamp
with a slack and heaving dirge.
It's not the song I minded,
just the silence when it was over.

THE TIME I CIRCUMVENTED U.S.-MEXICO BORDER PATROL TO AID THE REBELLION

One does not say, "Can you direct me
to the nearest Zapatista hideout?"

One resigns himself to a labyrinth
of mountain passes and quiet towns
where only the children let you ask questions.
I trade candy for answers.

I know I'm there
when the muzzle of an AK nudges me awake.

The scariest part is when they put you on a truck
headed for a location they would die to keep secret
and they don't blindfold you.

The village is like the others,
filled with constant work and slow laughter.
There are no masks, no leering shifty quiet.

Two hours in a room with roach motels
and air conditioning.

A woman enters with hips
twice as wide as her shoulders.
Says her name is Pilar.
Tree-trunk legs carry her frame
like it's filled with feathers.
Her wrinkled hand sets tamales
and a canteen in front of me.
The chair creaks as she sits.

It takes a minute before I get it.
She's the one they sent to talk to me.

I ask to see Marcos.
She shouts outside, *Marcos! Ven aqui.*
An 8-year-old boy in an AC/DC shirt enters.

No. *The Subcomandante*, I say.
Is she really this dense?

In perfect English, she answers,
Oh, my mistake.

She takes a balaclava out of her pocket
and puts it over the boy's head.
He giggles a little. She shushes him.

What's wrong? she says.
Don't you recognize a Jew in Germany when you see one?

I tell her I came a long way, please just—
Don't you recognize a Tutsi in Rwanda?

I tell her I have money. She needs money, doesn't she?
What about a Gypsy in Poland? A homosexual in Texas—

Enough!
I slam a fist against the plate,
sending a tamale into the wall.

She gets up and heads for the door.
I came to join you, I say.

She stops, turns, and asks me where I'm from.
I tell her.

Then you must have seen single mothers
alone on the bus at one in the morning.
I tell her I have.

You want to join us? she says.
Then go and sit with them.

TO MY ZOMBIE-KILLING EX-BOYFRIEND: A BREAKUP LETTER

Once,
you scratched my nickname into two bullets
and handed one to me, saying,
Honeybee, if the time comes,
these are for us.
So I scratched "Thumper" into two bullets
and handed one to you.

When the shit came down,
I ran out of ammo.
All I had left was my Thumper and my Honeybee
but I didn't use them.
Instead, I wrapped my hands
around the last zombie's throat
and squeezed until the snarl faded from its face—
a process I like to call "going bareback."

I asked you if it was wrong that I enjoyed it.
But you just grabbed the back of my head,
hard enough to give me that good pain,
and pulled my face into yours.

I couldn't be this way
if I were with a lady.

Sometimes I think about Rosaline
and how she had this idea
that there was something inside of those things,
that was still human.

She said the more I killed,
the more I reminded her of one of them.
We fought about it
up until the day that zedhead
closed its jaws on her neck,
and her pretty eyes
blew me that long kiss goodnight.

Around her, I always took point.
I was last to sleep, first to rise.
I never gave her two bullets to set aside.
When she asked me
what we should do if the time comes,

I told her I wouldn't let that happen.

But you and me—
we slept in shifts, took turns at the wheel,
had loud sex in wide open spaces,
and when we fought
I bit my lip with the snap
of each chambered round,
pressed my back against yours
and fed on your rage.

It gave me clarity.

But yesterday
I saw a zombie child
pet the coat of a gray coyote
while the two of them shared the meat
from their human kill.

Thumper,
I'm sorry I ended it. But I'm tired
of being as vicious as my enemies.

If it's any consolation, those things
are all around me now
and all I've got is your name
waiting in my chamber.

WATCHING FALLEN BRIDGES

We're on the overpass where I work
shouting warnings at commuters and you
dangle from the edge, part time.

While I wonder why no one listens,
why they'd rather pitch themselves into freefall
than program new directions,
you lean—

chest out, arms back, as much of you tilting
over the freeway as possible.
There is a chemistry between you two
that makes you say things like,
Wouldn't I look stunning in a ten-car pileup?

Every time your eyes trace the tail lights
carving their frowns in the air, your grip weakens,
and I wonder if today's the day
you're going to get all Doppler shifty.

I don't want to know what it's like
to be alone in a lighthouse when the power goes out
and there's nothing but fireflies and votive candles
to keep the signal alive.

Stay a minute longer
up here with the mad gulls and the gossip
of the cell antenna.

On the ground, the air is stale and still.
Weathervanes become liars.
Wind chimes are just lazy xylophones.
Ideal conditions for smoke ring parties
where everyone speaks in weightless zeroes.

Here, the storms force you to speak fluent cannonball.
Surefire eddies strip away everything
that isn't bolted to your frame.

Stay until they kick up again.
Don't leave before you know
which parts of you are jagged and porous,
and which are aerodynamic.

TO PAN

Secretly, you envy the defeated Spartan,
axe buried in his throat, fingering the grass
in a field in Elysium.

You no longer look at nymphs in untouched meadows
and see foot races dying to begin.
They are getting too fast for you.

There is a night you hope for,
that you know will never come,
when your pipes are just the wind
and the song curves when the reeds bend.

You ache for that last sip.
You think about the water beneath the lily pads
and the fetid calm that must lie there.

It's stronger every day, the whisper
coaxing the mirth from the glen.

You will know it's time to leave
when the scent of barley wine fades
against the sweetness of the hemlock.

TO NIGHTFALL

Scientists are still trying to figure out
how you are drawing the universe in on itself
despite being nothing
but a blackness that Cleopatra
would lick a sandal for.

When it's warm out
we sit in you,
mouths and eyes open,
like the fingers of a glove.

Over the years, people have stopped
diving from rocks into dark lakes.
There is something about empty ledges
that makes you want to wring the sleep out of us.

At the end,
when the sun grows
and the days lengthen,
we will lie berm-side
and lake-chilled,
pores closing,
trapping you in.

PART THREE

MACH 1

I watch the space shuttle take off
while my third-grade teacher explains
that its rockets are giant controlled explosions
pointed at the ground,
sending the crew and cargo up
at seven hundred and sixty miles per hour.
Mach 1.
That, he says, is how we escape the earth.

I watch, transfixed on the TV
as a plume of gas flares from the engine,
causing it to break from its housing,
and alter the shuttle's attitude
relative to air flow so that, technically,
Challenger did not explode.
Rather, it disintegrated
from aerodynamic force.

Since then, I have had insomnia.

I am told it's because I think too much.
I have a friend who used to worry
about all the best questions.
Now, she takes Fluoxetine
to inhibit her serotonin re-uptake
and laugh at all the worst jokes.

My mother walks with a cane
even though her new hip is made
from the same material as the space shuttle.
Open her coffin in a thousand years
and her hip will still be reusable.

An old friend told me his life
was a controlled explosion.
He turned to a cult leader's god
when methamphetamines failed
to get him high enough
to escape the gravity of Earth.

I am tired of seeing us lying open
on the tables of watchmakers.

I am tired of men with iron lapels
and expensive answers
making better gears to grind us back into dust.

I am standing at the edge of the Earth,
staring at the drop-off into space
and I am scared
that the greatest minds of my generation
are lining up to sell me plastic wings.

Sometimes my insomnia gets so bad,
I can't sleep unless I listen to the static on the TV.

When Challenger disintegrated,
only the cargo and crew were lost.
The rockets were designed to survive.
They kept going.
Kept pushing up, away
from all things human.

That night I asked my father,
Dad, where do you go when you die?
He told me to ask God.
When I cried, he held me tight.
It's okay, David.
It's all right.
Sometimes
you just think too much.

THE PASSION OF THE CHRIST ON OPENING NIGHT

When I see the line wrapping twice
around Mexico City's largest IMAX theater,
I expect holy water at the door
and the teenagers at the booth
to place the tickets on our waiting tongues.

Had I won the coin toss,
we'd be halfway through *Kill Bill*.

Instead, the lights go down
and I remember why I used to be afraid of the dark.
At bed time I cursed my father's light switch powers.
One flick and he turned the hamper
into a caged animal, and the branches
into fingers tapping at my window.

Tonight, a director with a house in Malibu
turns rabbis with thick beards and big noses
into the only monsters parents still believe in—
not to teach us about love everlasting,
but to coil his mitts around our fears
and squeeze out all the tiny pesos they're worth.

As children, we repeated the Lord's Prayer
to silence the voices coming from the closet.
Today, we use the hum of the projector.

We pay for a beam to cut the darkness
so we can believe
someone upstairs knows the story.

When the credits roll,
a man stands, says he's a priest,
and asks to lead us in prayer.

Every pair of hands folds.
A wave of bowing heads ripples through the crowd.
Alien vs. Predator should have started five minutes ago,
but the manager's eyes are pressed into slits.
Employees with brooms and Hefty bags, in unison, sing:
En el Nombre del Padre, del Hijo y del Espíritu Santo. . . .

When they say *amen*,
this is not a theater. It is not a bedroom.
It is the opposite of what Christ found in Jerusalem:
a marketplace transformed into a temple.

A long time ago I learned
that ceilings are hard of hearing,
so I stopped begging them for answers,
but tonight I ask,
"Is this it?
Does all our light and warmth
come from burning our enemy's scriptures?"

The answer is a worker
admitting his trespasses as tears tap
at the inside of his trash can.

Watching him is like watching a movie.
It is light shining through a negative.

Leaving the theater,
an old woman drags an oxygen tank
while rosary beads sway from her walker.
When I hold the door for her,
she asks me why I didn't pray.

All I can say is,
No soy de este lugar.
Sólo vine a ver.

I am not from this place.
I only came to watch.

KUNG FU IS DEAD

Lost in David Carradine's crystalline stare,
my grandfather would torque into
left hooks and palm thrusts
matching the choreography as far
as the La-Z-Boy allowed.

Same look on his face in the garden—
breathing through his teeth, adding a bite mark
to his lips every time he pruned a limb too thin.

The time I refused to help him,
he looked at me like I was a crop circle,
wondering if it was a joke
or time to get the shotgun.

Manual labor can either be
cross-training for your dignity
or steroids for your spite.

Picking the zucchini a week early would teach him.

The sons and daughters of field hands
expect dinner well prepared— it's their allowance
for mastering precision window shopping
and haiku wish lists. A daily reward
for sharing the fireplace
when Christmas comes with its eyes on its shoes,
muddied in the soil of the company farm.

But that night,
the stir-fry was tender as a steel-belted radial.
They ground it in their jaws like cows on cud.
There is a very special fear reserved

for when people glare at you
while chewing very slowly.

The intervention was swift.
They made cut-outs from my summer vacation
in the shapes of all their unfinished tasks.

I would learn to soften in the sun
and to press myself thin
against the hand-me-down anvils of work.

They planned, pitching their voices
so I'd hear from the TV room.
Listening to them, he tapped his cigarette,
sighed like he'd heard it all before,
and turned on Kung Fu.

Carradine dug a toe in the dirt,
drew back a fist, and panned a closing brigade.
Knowing full well he'd fall in a hailstorm
if any of this were real,
we listed toward the screen,
breathless, fearless,
waiting for the blow.

EMISSARY

We inch forward through the mall's clogged arteries.
Passing Hot Topic and its employees
in full zombie makeup, she says,
Don't give me a funeral.

As a drop in the bucket
of the unpayable debt I owe her,
I don't avoid the subject.

Her voice tears open an old envelope
and the instructions file out.

A little get-together is fine.
Aunt Carole wants to make a Jell-O mold
of a frizzy-haired lady hunched over a walker;
she can knock herself out.

But no quaking organ.
No priest outfitting the bedridden years
with prosthetic meaning. No flowers.
Leave 'em in the ground where we both belong.

Elevator doors slide shut.
My iced coffee weeps into my hands.
Escalators drag entire families
to a glowing subterranean archway.

I nod, *yeah sure,*
knowing that when the time comes—
when they show up cradling their fractures,
looking to me for the ritual resetting—
I will meet them with a noose around my tongue,
and excuses carpet bombing my backbone.

Her eyes narrow.
She knows my jellyfish routine,
my perforated constitution.
I don't know what memory she's pulling from,
what emissary sits for me at the table
where she surrenders her trust.

Later, I will promise out loud,
and the time-release capsule of resolve
she slipped me before I made my own lunches
will spring its first leak.

Now, I tell her to meet me in the food court.
On the way to the bathroom
(where I am going to sit alone and breathe
until my edges stop blurring), I turn.

As the escalator lifts her to the next floor,
she looks into the bloom of the skylights
and accepts their soft coronation.

THE CURSE OF THE DRINKING CLASSES

They say you died behind the bar,
after doing this for so long
that you could mix a Black 'n Tan
with both hands in baseball gloves.
Some nights, they say the fridge locks itself
and a cool breeze paces
between the bathroom and the dartboard.

Nice story.
But it took a pint glass sailing into a wall
and a dish rag gliding over the counter on its own
before I believed in you.

I come here because it's not like other Irish pubs,
in that the owner is actually Irish.
You know from the picture of the Queen of England
picking her nose during a Remembrance Day parade
and from the Oscar Wilde quote on the door:

"Work is the curse of the drinking classes."

A hundred years ago,
this place was pissing distance from a coal mine.
Both belonged to the same man,
someone who taxed taut shoulders by day,
and by night, the love of the glass.

Today,
bank tellers and music teachers
use pink slips as coasters.
Programmers of dead languages
trap farts in the stools and pray for the clock
to stop fanning the room.

The tables are coarse with their elbow-shaped divots
and warped from the weight of their stories,
as tragic as they are unsolicited.
I don't mind talking to them,
just looking in their eyes and seeing meteors
vaporizing in the atmosphere.

You made your living eight inches from their faces,
feeling the warmth of whiskey fumes rising from their breath.
They are the reason the hardest drinks are called "spirits."
They linger in places where souls aren't free to rest.

Maybe you think you did them a favor,
dying facedown in a puddle of Jameson
but staying overtime to clean up after them.

But where will they go
when word gets out about you?
When the place becomes the Shangri-La of tourist traps,
driving them out with player pianos,
paranormal trivia night, and ten-dollar covers?

Every day you came to work
your body was owned by your employer.
But now that your soul is your only possession,
don't let him have that, too.
Not to say you have to go to heaven or hell,
just that you can't stay here.

OLVIDAR

Quiero decirte the story de mi tia.
It begins con ella quando estaba alone
El unico voice of reason.
The only todo. El unico.

I want to tell you la historia de mi aunt.
It begins con ella quando estaba corriendo
por los montanas con mucho
peso en su espada, corriendo mas alta, mas alta.
Termina in el hospital forgetting todo
su Ingles, word for palabra.

Quiero decirte a story that begins with a woman
running through los mountains
con mucho weight on her back.
Running higher y higher and mas alta.

I want to tell you a story that begins with mountains
and ends with mi tia en el hospital
forgetting todo her English word by word.

She spent eight anos en un cuarto de a hospital
finding patterns in the stucco walls
while the ones in her mind faded,
became mas darker y mas oscuro.

Her historia begins con immigration and ends with
the flowers I brought her once a year.

No pude understand her words, but I always knew
her meaning. When she said, No puedo verlos,
I knew to move the flowers to her bedside.

She learned to speak simply around me.
As she forgot su Ingles, I forgot mi Espanol.

I lost it to a world of dead tongues
donde todo is translated before it is understood.
Tambien personas.
Even people.

People, translated.
Originals
forgotten.

Cuando she lost her English to eight years
of staring into off-white stucco walls,
I lost my Spanish to time y neglect.

I am left con language como poltergeist
that tugs at my feet cada noche
and makes sounds I don't want to admit I can hear.

I remember her failed attempts at conversation
when she groped in the dark for my name.
Her palabras became el meaningless wash
of television static or refrigerator buzz.
One de muchos en una chorus de empty white noises.

English colonized my mind.
Oigo Espanol solo in mi dreams of the dead
where I decipher the tongues
de su footsteps in the hallway
y the scratches at the door.

Uso una language I cannot speak
but somehow understand,
whose words I do not remember
pero no puedo olvidar.
I cannot seem to completely forget.

I want to tell you the story of my aunt,
but all I have is a poor translation.

BLANE

Blane would coil a fist in barbed wire
and go looking for arguments
with it hidden in his pocket.
He'd shoot BBs into traffic,
drive thumbtacks into his neck.
He once dissected a living guinea pig
with a number 2 pencil.

But he didn't get arrested
until he was standing on the street,
folding sheets of colored paper
into birds of prey,
into horses,
into a herd of giraffes
surrounded by a zoo of family pets.
Palms turned upward to the passersby:
Dollar for a dog?
Cigarette for a cat?
And for that, they put him in a home
for people with mental illness,
and there, I was his counselor.

Blane was born with a problem
but I gave him a disease
and a treatment
of daily mood-stabilization cocktails
of Lithium, Wellbutrin, Effexor, and Prozac
mixed with an hour a day
of actual human contact.

For the first few weeks of it
he was silent:

hugging his knees,
eyes on the carpet,
headphones blasting
to drown out the world,
folded in the corner like an origami oven.
Only a matter of time before it catches.
His only companions, the sheets of paper
he creased and tucked.

One day he comes to me
asking for more medication
because the room is spinning.
The ceiling has turned to Jell-O
and the beehive in the wall is reading his mind.

He wants more medication
because the faces in the darkness
have been looking through him
to the blind spot
where the ape-man laughs at him.
He hasn't slept in a week
because he's got these friends of his
scratched into the backs of his eyelids.

He keeps them open with coffee grounds
in his mouth like tobacco chew
and needles in the tender spots between his fingers.
He stays awake making a world without human beings
out of creased and folded sheets.

He makes birds of prey
and construction paper dragons
with tissue talons,
lace fire, and cotton smoke.

He's asking me for more medication
but I don't want to be the muzzle

in the back of Cobain's throat.
I don't want to be the syringe
buried in the veins of Bill Burroughs.
And I don't want to be the rocks in the pockets
of Virginia Woolf's overcoat.

I tell him, no.

A few weeks later
they send him to lock down
for tattooing his palms
with a Bic and a safety pin.

Years later, I see him
standing on the same street.
Dollar for a dog?
Smoke for a cat?
He hands me a bird of prey.
I dig in my pockets but he stops me,
No, Dave, this one's on me.

MR. WHATCHAMACALLIT

Mr. Whatchamacallit points to a box of tiny white things
shaped like bite-sized sponges and asks,
W-w-w-what's that thing called?
I pass it to him.
It's shredded wheat, Brandon. Can you say that?
Sometimes he can.
Sometimes I read him poetry instead.
Most days his lips just twist around words that aren't there.
He is like a cat pouncing on a shadow.
I get ten dollars an hour to keep him clawing at nothing.

At five o'clock my shift is up,
but Brandon lives in a moment he can't escape.
The doctors say he has aphasia
but it's more like a splinter in the brain
between names and things—
between cats and four-legged furry beasts—
between shredded wheat and tiny white sponges—
between poetry and words that vacuum your breath away
leaving an old soul in its place.

Today we're playing a game.
We're using poetry to remember things.
I read him this poem where a horse is the narrator.
It pulls the carriage of a slave trader.
Only it doesn't know the word "carriage"
so it says "the wood box that sits on four rolling circles."
On good days Brandon remembers words for things.
On bad days he gets stuck
in these moments he can't escape.

I remember reading in his file
about the day his white power march
crossed a gay pride parade.

If the skinheads were a marching band,
Brandon was their baton twirler,
curling boys around baseball bats
for blowing kisses in the wrong direction.

It's already five o'clock.
I just want to get through the poem,
but Brandon wants to say something.
His eyes are searchlights
scanning an empty night
for the right words.

I want it to be an apology.
So I read about the horse.
It pulls the carriage of a slave trader.
Only it doesn't know the word "carriage,"
just a box on circles.
It doesn't know the word "trader,"
just a man who sells things.
It doesn't know the word "slave,"
just a man with a head heavier than a cannonball.

I read this and Brandon cries very softly.
He points to a picture of a man's back,
ripped with jagged lashes, and says,
Looks like sh-sh-sh-shredded wheat.

Brandon was not a skinhead.
He was someone who used a bowie knife
to scare all flesh his own shade of pale,
and to cut the devil out of men who lie with men.
I am not a counselor.
I am someone who gets ten dollars an hour
to listen to a man trapped in a poem
that never ends.

LOST AT THE JIANGUOMEN METRO STATION

Inspired by Mark Leong's photography collection entitled "China Obscura"

My pupils shrink to points
as they dart from floor to sky.
I turn and my friends are gone.
It's just the ducks in the window, the train depot
and the alley where they slaughter sheep:
their necks like popped bottle tops,
their noses drying in the sun.
I'm swept in a current
of shoulders and glares.
Faces speak in tongues.
There's the smell of wet metal.
Knives brown with rust.
The butcher stares at me:
watches me watching the lambs
stiffen and cool.
He eats lunch with wool in his hair
and clippers on his lap.
The day is jointless and bright.

When night falls on Beijing,
the heat of the day lingers
in ten thousand cupped hands.

I WANT YOU TO TOUCH ME THERE, THERE, THERE, THERE, AND THERE

There is thinking about you.
Then, there is touching myself
while I imagine that you
hold my eyes shut and slap me
until I see the aurora borealis bloom inside my head.
I will try very hard to hold this image steady in my mind
as I tongue the point of a turnip.
I want you to touch me there, there, there, there, and there.
I want you to read this and imagine where "there" is.
There is thinking about you,
and then there is choking myself with turnips
partially naked as I gaze into your status update.
I want you to hear "partially"
and imagine a necktie and a rose petal
doing their best to cover us.
I want you to touch me there, there, there, there, and there.
I want you to say, "There, there,"
as you snatch my turnips away from me
and brush my lips with the cherry
of a cigarette.
Yes, I went there.
Yes, this is that there.
There is what happens to me
when you leave the room for five minutes.
There is a hunger like a trench in the belly of the sun.
Then there is me wanting the day off
and a teddy bear with your smell clinging to its fur.

CONTRABAND

He sat pretzel-legged in a ring of burning incense.
Crown folded from a KFC bucket.
Necklace of painted chicken bones.

His sign read:
Will Give Spiritual Council for Drugs.

Maybe *Can't help you, man* was starting to feel hackneyed.
Maybe I was tired of talking to statues with pleated slacks
and framed degrees.
Maybe I was just sick of it—the icy void.

I passed him the dime bag
like feeding a quarter into an arcade game.

It's okay, bro. Don't feel bad.

His voice was a pack-a-day Geiger counter.
When he looked at me, all real-time and searching,
I checked my breastplates for windowpanes.

Whatchu wanna know?

I wanted to know why I can't leave the house
without some Super Bowl-worthy pep talk,
why when I talk to a lover
I lose my place on the script,
and where I get off hogging all this oxygen.

But said:
"I . . . I . . ."

He clasped my head
in a two-handed vise
and whispered:

Your flaws make you.
What're you gonna do without 'em,
play bingo?

I've seen him a hundred times since then.
Total scam artist.
He tells everyone the same thing.

HOW MAY I HELP YOU?

I write poetry because I can't tell you the truth to your face.
I need to be ten feet away, on a stage.
I can't look into your eyes unless mine
are blinded by spotlights
and I need a mic stand between us
in order to tell you that I love you.
I can scream it into your face
but I can't whisper it in your ear
because in another life,
you buried my ancestors in riverbeds.
When we tried to run, you burned off our feet.
When we tried to speak,
you fed our sisters' tongues to us.
We wanted nothing more than to plunge our fists
into your chest, rip out your heart and laugh.
You piece of shit.
Don't leave me.

How may I help you?

I write poetry because it's never convenient
to tell you that we were once joined at the chest,
spinning at the center of a black hole,
and that our pulses beat at the pace
of the changes in the equinoxes.
What am I supposed to tell you?
We were brothers before the universe was born;
by the way, do you want fries with that?

How may I help you?

How can I help you
when we have shackled our mother
to the rafters in the attic
and we are slowly killing her
by sticking needles into her esophagus?
We have turned her throat into a pincushion.
Her eyes flutter like upturned beetles.
We need to talk about this.
We can't afford to live at opposite ends of town.
You can't afford to trade diamonds for lap dances
and I can't afford to clean out the president's ears
with sniper bullets.

I never told you this
but as a kid I was thrown from my bike
into oncoming traffic
then rushed to intensive care.
For an hour my heart stopped and started
like a joke no one remembers how to tell.
My mind rose to a hole in the ceiling.

What Mom and Dad said was true.
When you die,
you and God sit in a theater
and watch the movie of your life.

Scene 1
was you and me inventing language
by playing Scrabble in a flaming chariot
with solid gold Daytons on its wheels.

Scene 2
was me digging in your stomach
with a switch-blade
to find the teeth
you stole from my head.

Scene 3
was me getting a job at Burger King.

Scene 4
was our mother bracing herself
on our shoulders
as she learned to walk again.

Scene 5
was me asking,
How may I help you?
And you answering,
You already have.

BROKEN ENGLISH

I once had a brother
who saw the world the way he wished it could be.

When me and my friends were in the sandbox
building battle bunkers and rocket launchers,
he built schools out of Legos,
hospitals out of popsicle sticks.
In manic fits he'd fit together
Lincoln Logs and Super Glue
into libraries.

From the age of eight,
every time he blew out his birthday candles
he wished for a DeLorean
to travel back in time in
so he could throw himself
in front of the bullet
meant for Malcolm.

I once had a brother who spoke
the way poets wish they could dream.
He made kindergarten seem like Harvard,
and schoolyard fights
seem like tight-puckered first kisses.

I remember this one time
he caught a pop fly with his eyes closed.

I remember this one time
he picked our mother a dozen roses.

I remember this one time
he swung from a tree

by a noose,
kicking at the stars
like riding an invisible bicycle.

He took the threads from the rope
and made me a four-armed sweater,
two extra for the wings he said I'd grow
when I use my words to teach myself
the things I've always known.

From ear to ear they slit his throat.

They gave him a second mouth
through which he forced his poems out.
But I never learned to speak his language.

I never learned to speak Spanish.
I never learned to speak Hindi.
I never learned to speak Farsi,
French, Portuguese, Russian,
Polish, Tagalog, Tongan,
Tai, Mandarin, Pawnee,
Japanese, Swahili, Arabic,
or Pidgin Liberian.

Today, I pull at my tongue
and pound on my throat
to make my bold-faced lies come out
until all I have is this broken English.

I want to see him again.
I want us to remove our tongues
and speak with hands and eyes,
laughter and breath.
I want to forget the person
I am trying to become, and forgive myself
for being the person I know I am.

COMMUNION

Father Junípero Serra, founder of seven of California's twenty-one missions, once wrote, "that spiritual fathers should punish their sons, the Indians, with blows appears to be as old as the conquest of the Americas; so general in fact that the saints do not seem to be any exception to the rule." Today, his statue stands in Hillsborough, California with a finger pointing westward.

If a person looks hard enough
they'll find they have a black market contact.
Seventy-two hours after finding mine,
I held a brick of plastic explosive.
It felt like Play-Doh.
Something that would let me
reshape the world as I saw fit.

As far back as I can tell,
the bones of kings have been crawling
from the jewels in their tombs
to ghostwrite history, and rub erasers
against the diary pages of saints.

It didn't matter to me
that there were no more baptisms at gunpoint—
no more undiscovered lands west of Hillsborough.
I wanted Father Serra's stone finger on my mantle.

I climbed his statue
and found a notch in his hand
I could fill with Play-Doh.
It was September 4, 2001.

Seven days later,
the TV was baring its white teeth
and clawing at a fresh cloud of ash and steel.

It was the beginning of something winding and hideous.

I wondered who these children were
making more rubble to play with.
Predictably, Father Serra sat dumbly
pointing at me.

For once, he was right.

Sitting in a row boat
I dropped the Play-Doh over the side
and watched it shrink into the depths.

I listened to the air and water—
an armchair mathematician
looking for patterns in static.
I wanted our rheumatic grudges
to take their places among the shipwrecks.
I wanted to bury our weapons and lies
but had only my own.

ACKNOWLEDGMENTS

Thanks to Victoria Scott and Jennifer Gigantino for their editorial support; to my teachers Micah Perks, David Sullivan, Darrah Cloud, and Neil Landau; to Mike McGee, Lucia Misch, Tristissima, Kat Dietrich, Chris Bundy, and all the poets in my life with their eyes forward; and to my mother, father, and sister for their prudent advice, tech support, and love.

ABOUT THE AUTHOR

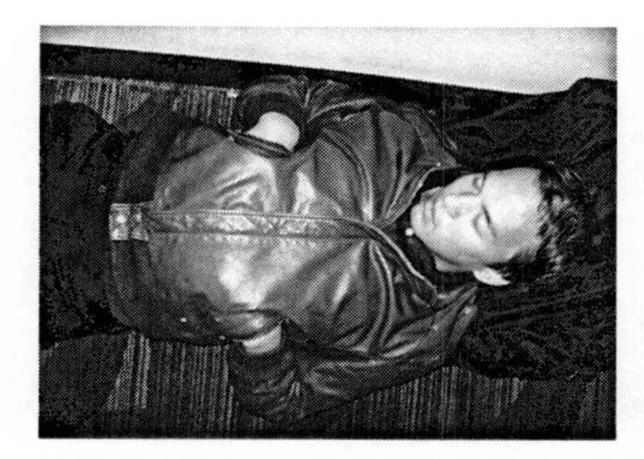

David Perez is a recipient of the Arts Council Silicon Valley Fellowship for Literary Arts. He tours regularly throughout the United States and Canada, and has competed at the Individual World Poetry Slam and the National Poetry Slam. He currently lives in San Jose, California where he teaches youth and adult creative writing workshops and hosts various poetry and performance art events. This is his first book.

www.thedavidperez.com

NEW WRITE BLOODY BOOKS FOR 2011

DEAR FUTURE BOYFRIEND
A Write Bloody reissue of Cristin O'Keefe Aptowicz's first book of poetry

HOT TEEN SLUT
A Write Bloody reissue of Cristin O'Keefe Aptowicz's second book of poetry about her time writing for porn

WORKING CLASS REPRESENT
A Write Bloody reissue of Cristin O'Keefe Aptowicz's third book of poetry

OH, TERRIBLE YOUTH
A Write Bloody reissue of Cristin O'Keefe Aptowicz's fourth book of poetry about her terrible youth

38 BAR BLUES
A collection of poems by C.R .Avery

WORKIN' MIME TO FIVE
Humor by Derrick Brown

REASONS TO LEAVE THE SLAUGHTER
New poems by Ben Clark

YESTERDAY WON'T GOODBYE
New poems by Brian Ellis

WRITE ABOUT AN EMPTY BIRDCAGE
New poems by Elaina M. Ellis

THESE ARE THE BREAKS
New prose by Idris Goodwin

BRING DOWN THE CHANDELIERS
New poems by Tara Hardy

THE FEATHER ROOM
New poems by Anis Mojgani

LOVE IN A TIME OF ROBOT APOCALYPSE
New poems by David Perez

THE NEW CLEAN
New poems by Jon Sands

THE UNDISPUTED GREATEST WRITER OF ALL TIME
New poems by Beau Sia

SUNSET AT THE TEMPLE OF OLIVES
New poems by Paul Suntup

GENTLEMAN PRACTICE
New work by Buddy Wakefield

HOW TO SEDUCE A WHITE BOY IN TEN EASY STEPS
New poems by Laura Yes Yes

OTHER WRITE BLOODY BOOKS (2003 - 2010)

STEVE ABEE, GREAT BALLS OF FLOWERS (2009)
New poems by Steve Abee

EVERYTHING IS EVERYTHING (2010)
New poems by Cristin O'Keefe Aptowicz

CATACOMB CONFETTI (2010)
New poems by Josh Boyd

BORN IN THE YEAR OF THE BUTTERFLY KNIFE (2004)
Poetry collection (1994-2004) by Derrick Brown

I LOVE YOU IS BACK (2006)
Poetry compilation (2004-2006) by Derrick Brown

SCANDALABRA (2009)
New poetry compilation by Derrick Brown

DON'T SMELL THE FLOSS (2009)
New Short Fiction Pieces By Matty Byloos

THE BONES BELOW (2010)
New poems by Sierra DeMulder

THE CONSTANT VELOCITY OF TRAINS (2008)
New poems by Lea C. Deschenes

HEAVY LEAD BIRDSONG (2008)
New poems by Ryler Dustin

UNCONTROLLED EXPERIMENTS IN FREEDOM (2008)
New poems by Brian Ellis

CEREMONY FOR THE CHOKING GHOST (2010)
New poems by Karen Finneyfrock

POLE DANCING TO GOSPEL HYMNS (2008)
Poems by Andrea Gibson

CITY OF INSOMNIA (2008)
New poems by Victor D. Infante

THE LAST TIME AS WE ARE (2009)
New poems by Taylor Mali

IN SEARCH OF MIDNIGHT: THE MIKE MCGEE HANDBOOK OF AWESOME (2009)
New poems by Mike McGee

OVER THE ANVIL WE STRETCH (2008)
New poems by Anis Mojgani

ANIMAL BALLISTICS (2009)
New poems by Sarah Morgan

NO MORE POEMS ABOUT THE MOON (2008)
NON-Moon poems by Michael Roberts

MILES OF HALLELUJAH (2010)
New poems by Rob "Ratpack Slim" Sturma

SPIKING THE SUCKER PUNCH (2009)
New poems by Robbie Q. Telfer

RACING HUMMINGBIRDS (2010)
New poems by Jeanann Verlee

LIVE FOR A LIVING (2007)
New poems by Buddy Wakefield

WRITE BLOODY ANTHOLOGIES

THE ELEPHANT ENGINE HIGH DIVE REVIVAL (2009)
Poetry by Buddy Wakefield, Derrick Brown,
Anis Mojgani, Shira Erlichman and many more!

THE GOOD THINGS ABOUT AMERICA (2009)
An illustrated, un-cynical look at our American Landscape. Various authors.
Edited by Kevin Staniec and Derrick Brown

JUNKYARD GHOST REVIVAL (2008)
Poetry by Andrea Gibson, Buddy Wakefield, Anis Mojgani,
Derrick Brown, Robbie Q, Sonya Renee and Cristin O'Keefe Aptowicz

**THE LAST AMERICAN VALENTINE:
ILLUSTRATED POEMS TO SEDUCE AND DESTROY (2008)**
24 authors, 12 illustrators team up for a collection of non-sappy love poetry.
Edited by Derrick Brown

LEARN THEN BURN (2010)
Anthology of poems for the classroom. Edited by Tim Stafford and Derrick Brown.

LEARN THEN BURN TEACHER'S MANUAL (2010)
Companion volume to the *Learn Then Burn* anthology. Includes lesson plans and worksheets for educators.
Edited by Tim Stafford and Molly Meacham.

WWW.WRITEBLOODY.COM

WRITEBLOODY
QUALITY AMERICAN BOOKS

CPSIA information can be obtained at www.ICGtesting.com
Printed in the USA
LVOW06s1852050814

397633LV00004B/203/P